JAVASCRIPT

QuickStart Guide

The Simplified Beginner's Guide To JavaScript

Martin Mihajlov

in partnership with

Edition # 1 – Updated : May 5, 2016

Cover Illustration and Design: Katie Poorman, Copyright © 2016 by ClydeBank Media LLC
Interior Design: Katie Poorman, Copyright © 2016 by ClydeBank Media LLC

ClydeBank Media LLC
P.O Box 6561
Albany, NY 12206
Printed in the United States of America

Copyright © 2015
ClydeBank Media LLC
www.clydebankmedia.com
All Rights Reserved

ISBN-13 : 978-0-9963667-3-1

contents

BEFORE YOU START READING,
DOWNLOAD YOUR FREE DIGITAL ASSETS!

Be sure to visit the URL below on your computer
or mobile device to access the free digital asset files
that are included with your purchase of this book.

These digital assets will compliment the material
in the book and are referenced throughout the text.

DOWNLOAD YOURS HERE:

www.clydebankmedia.com/javascript-assets

1

Introduction

HTML is not very smart. It lets people look at text and images and allows them to move to other pages where they will do more of the same, but what adds the intelligence to a web page is *JavaScript*. It makes the website more engaging, effective, and useful by letting pages respond to their visitors as they interact with the content.

This book assumes that you already know how to use HTML to specify web page structure and content. It is also beneficial if you are familiar with how pages are styled with *CSS*. If this is the case, then you are ready to make it more dynamic and interactive with JavaScript. Without HTML and CSS, JavaScript will not do you much good. They are the three fundamental pillars of the web page: structure, presentation and behavior.

This book begins with an introduction to JavaScript and programming in general. Step-by-step, it explores the building blocks of programming logic as they exist in JavaScript. It efficiently builds on these fundamentals to introduce interaction and then moves into slightly more advanced territory with functions and objects. Finally, it introduces the *DOM* model and shows how to effectively control the browser and all its content.

What is JavaScript?

JavaScript is the scripting language of the web. Its sole purpose is to add interactivity to pages. In addition to interactivity, modern versions of JavaScript can also be used to load and parse information from external sources or even the website's users. JavaScript is essentially a piece of programming code embedded in the HTML structure of a web page. When the web browser reads this code, it activates a built-in interpreter that understands how to decipher this language and process its commands.

Although programming is involved during coding, JavaScript is not a programming language. In conventional web programming languages, like Java or .NET, the code has to be compiled before it is executed. Compiling means that the code has to be first sent to a special program that is run on the server. This program, also known as application server software, translates the code, creates the requested page and functionality and serves this back as HTML. Scripting languages like JavaScript are not compiled, but rather are interpreted on-the-fly. This means that no special software is involved as the user's own browser runs and executes the code as it is encountered.

The Birth & Growth of JavaScript

Initially called LiveScript, JavaScript was created by Brendan Eich in 1995 in just 10 days. It was meant to add scripting capabilities to the front-end interface of the Netscape Navigator browser. However, the language was so well received that within a year it was reverse-engineered and included in the Internet Explorer browser. By 2000 the language gained a lot of popularity and expanded significantly so it was submitted for standardization to the ECMA Committee.

Once it became standardized, JavaScript continued to grow in adoption and popularity in tandem with the expansion and growth of the World Wide Web and the refinements of the browsing experience. As a matter of fact, Google gave it a big push into the professional spotlight when it released Google Maps in 2005 and showed how JavaScript can be used to create exciting and dynamic interaction.

NOTE

JavaScript was created during a time when Java was a very popular language. Other than that, the languages are not related and have nothing in common except for basic programming logic.

Implementing JavaScript

As JavaScript code is part of the HTML document, you need to tell browsers when to run your scripts. There are two common options available when you want to include JavaScript in a web document, and in both cases you use the `<script>` element. The `<script>` tag tells the browser where the JavaScript code begins and where it ends within an HTML document. As such, this tag can be included either in the head or the body section of the page.

The first option is to place the code inline within the document structure. To do this, open a `<script>` tag, enter the JavaScript code, and then close with the `</script>` tag. You can theoretically leave the document like this, as almost all browsers assume that the scripting language between the <script> tags is JavaScript by default. Nevertheless, for maximum compatibility, extend this tag with the type attribute and the text/javascript value in order to instruct the browser how to exactly interpret the code.

```
<script type="text/javascript">
//A JavaScript comment
</script>
```

The second option is to load the JavaScript code from an external file into your HTML document. For this purpose you can use the `<script>` element again, but this time in addition to the type attribute you also include the URL to the external file in the src attribute of the `<script>` element. The external file must be a text-only file with the .js file extension that contains only pure JavaScript code without any HTML elements or CSS rules. For example, to call the external scripts.js file into your browser, use the following code:

NOTE

Script files are loaded in the order in which they are placed in the HTML code.

```
<script src="script.js" type="text/javascript">
</script>
```

Put JavaScript in an external file and include it in the web page when you like to share the functionalities across your entire web site. Otherwise, if you just need to add some local interactive behavior, embed the code within the page.

| 2 |
Fundamental Concepts

Generally, when we hear the term "programming" we immediately think of other people typing an incomprehensible string of letters and numbers. Programming looks like magic beyond the realm of mere mortals. Nevertheless, the concepts in programming are not difficult to grasp, as they always have real life applications. JavaScript, although it is not as simple as *HTML* or CSS, is not an overly complicated language. Unlike other languages, its "grammar" is more or less descriptive and intuitive making it a good fit for a first programming language. Basically, learning JavaScript is like learning a new language, but a new language that is similar to English. Once you learn the new words and understand how to put them together to form "sentences," you'll be good to go.

Syntax

Every language has its own characters and words that we arrange into a well-formed sentence according to a set of rules. These rules are also known as the language syntax, and it is the syntax that holds the language together and gives it meaning.

Before you start with some examples of JavaScript syntax, you must first set up the environment for JavaScript. As discussed previously, JavaScript code is always a part of the HTML code. Therefore, in order to work with JavaScript you first need to create a basic HTML document. So to start, open a text editor (like Notepad) and type in the HTML code for the most basic web page. In addition to the basic HTML tags, include a `<script>` element in the `<head>` section where you can start placing the JavaScript code.

```
<!doctype html>
<head>
<title>First Steps in JavaScript</title>
<script type="text/javascript">

</script>
</head>
<body>

</body>
</html>
```

Save this document as firststeps.html. If you are using Notepad, you have to remember to change the Save as Type field to 'All files.'

Statements

To express yourself in everyday common language, you use sentences as the basic form of communication. Similarly, in JavaScript you also form sentences to express your intentions, which are more formally called statements. A JavaScript sentence is the basic unit of communication, usually representing a single step in the program. And just like you put sentences together to express an opinion, you combine statements together to create a program.

Here is a simple example of what a JavaScript statement does. Between the opening and closing <script> tag of the html document, place the following text:

```
alert("JavaScript is starting to make a little sense.");
```

Further examples do not show the complete HTML code unless it is necessary. For initial reference your document should look like the following (*fg. 1*):

```
<!doctype html>
<head>
<title>First Steps in JavaScript</title>
<script type="text/javascript">
        alert("JavaScript is starting to make a little
sense.");
</script>
</head>
<body>

</body>
</html>
```

You can save the firsteps.html document and open it in a web browser. Once the page opens, you get an alert window with the message "*JavaScript is starting to make a little sense.*"

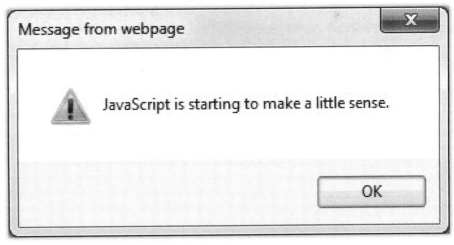

fg. 1 : Alert Window

Now that you know what the effect is, go back to the JavaScript statement and interpret it into common language so it makes more sense.

```
alert("JavaScript is starting to
make a little sense.");
```

JavaScript statements are instructions that are executed by the web browser. The statement starts with a command, presented by a keyword. The keyword identifies the action that needs to be performed. In this case the keyword `alert` makes the web browser open a dialog box and display a message. If you just had the statement `alert();` the dialog box would have been empty, but in this case the statement consists of a specific input, the actual message text, also known as an ***argument***. Finally, just like every sentence ends with a period, a JavaScript sentence ends with a semicolon. The semicolon makes it clear that the statement is over, and once the interpreter executes it, it should move on to the next item.

Now you are ready to translate the JavaScript statement. Its plain English interpretation would be, "Open a dialog box and display the text *JavaScript is starting to make a little sense*' in that box."

Here is another JavaScript statement. In the `<script>` element replace the previous code with the following and preview it in a web browser to see the results (*fg. 2*):

```
document.write("<p>JavaScript is
starting to make a little sense.</
p>");
```

NOTE

When passing text arguments, use either double quote marks ("sense") or single quote marks ('sense') to present the text.

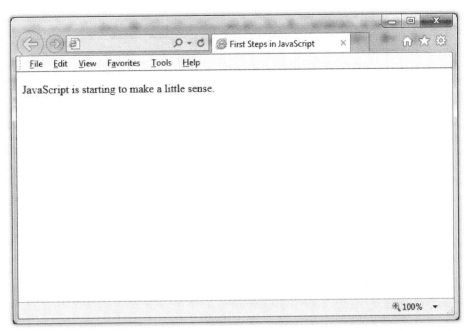

fg. 2 : Example of a document.write statement.

The previously empty document now has one paragraph of text. Following the previous interpretation of how JavaScript works and from the web browser results you can correctly assume that the `document.write` keyword commands the browser to write directly onto the web page. Similar to `alert()`, it writes whatever is placed between the opening and closing brackets.

Variables

One of the fundamental aspects of JavaScript, and any programming language in general, is the concept of variables. A variable is a way to declare and store information that can later be used. This information can vary with the circumstances, hence the name "variable."

Look at the following statement.

```
var name = "Martin";
```

In plain language this is the same as saying, "My name is Martin." The keyword var is JavaScript speak for "create a variable," or in a programming dialect, "declare a variable." What follows is the name of the variable, which can be anything you choose with certain limits. Assigning a value to the variable is done with the = sign, which is not immediately necessary, as this can happen later. You can declare an undefined variable in one statement and assign it a value in a later statement. For example:

```
var name;
name = "Martin";
```

NOTE

Although you can use almost anything for a variable name, it is wise to use names that are meaningful because it will help you and other programmers to better understand the written code.

As mentioned previously, variable names can be anything, like: name, abc, R2D2, with a few rules. Variable names can contain letters, numbers, dollar signs ($), or lower lines (_); other special characters are not allowed. Furthermore, a variable name cannot begin with a number, but any other allowed value is acceptable. Finally, variable names are case-sensitive, meaning that the interpreter in the web browser makes a distinction between uppercase and lowercase letters, making 'score' different from 'Score.'

Variable Types

Based on the type of data, variables come in different flavors. The three most basic types are number, string, and boolean. A number *variable* is represented by a numeric character. This variable can accept whole integers, negative integers and fractional integers. Numbers are frequently used in calculations, so our number variables are often included in mathematical operations. The following statement declares a variable named age and assigns it a value of 35.

```
var age = 35;
```

A *string* variable is used to represent any series of letters like words or sentences. Strings are represented as a series of characters enclosed within quotation marks with the quotation marks signaling to the interpreter that what follows is a string variable. JavaScript allows you to use either double quotes (") or single quote (') marks, but you have to be mindful to use the same type of quotation mark.

```
var location = "California";
```

A *boolean* variable is rather simple, as it can accept only one of two values: true or false. This variable is used when you create JavaScript programs that you want to intelligently react to user actions. This will be addressed in the next chapter.

User Variables

JavaScript would not be fun if it didn't allow you to share your thoughts and create or alter the variables directly. One of the simplest ways to "give" your input is to use the prompt() command. (*fg. 3*)

```
var name = prompt ("What is your name?", " ")
document.write(name);
```

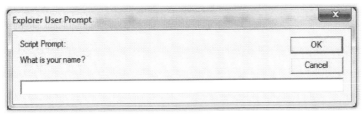

fg. 3 : A custom prompt dialog box

NOTE

"Calling" a variable to be presented on a web page is easy. Simply use the `document.write()` command.

The result of the `prompt()` command is a dialog box. Instead of just displaying a message like the alert dialog box, the prompt dialog box can also receive an answer. Hence, in the syntax for a prompt dialog box it is necessary to provide two arguments between the parentheses separated with a comma. The first argument

NOTE

Instead of `prompt()` you can also use the more formal `window.prompt` command.

is the prompt text that is displayed in the box, while the second argument is the default value for the text box, and consequently, the variable.

In the previous example, the prompt text displayed in the box is *'What is your name?'* and the default value presented in the box is empty, as there is obviously no content between the quotation marks. Once a user types something in the box and either clicks OK or presses the Enter key, the variable receives the value that was entered in the field. Consequently, the name will be displayed on the web page. Otherwise, if the user clicks on Cancel, presses the Esc key or closes the prompt box, the returned value will be empty and there will be no text on the screen.

Operators

Storing information in a variable is a first step. The beauty of programming is the ability to manipulate this information in many creative ways. For this, JavaScript provides different operators that allow you to modify data. An ***operator***, represented by a symbol or a word, can change one or more values into something else. The types of operators available are different based on the data type.

Mathematical Operators

The basic mathematical operators like addition (+), subtraction (-), multiplication (*) and division (/) are readily available in JavaScript. They can be used in independent statements or when declaring variables. For example (*fg. 4*), by "operating" with the variables `currentYear` and `yearofBirth`, you can determine the value of the variable age.

```
var currentYear = 2015;
var yearofBirth = 1979;
var age = currentYear - yearofBirth;
document.write(age);
```

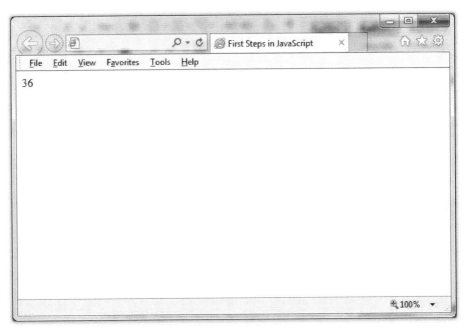

fg. 4 : Using variables to calculate age.

Mathematical operators, specifically the addition operator, combine two or more strings. This process of combining strings is called concatenation. In the following example (*fg. 5*) :

```
var firstName = "Martwan";
var lastName = "Jenkins";
var fullName = firstName+lastName;
document.write(fullName);
```

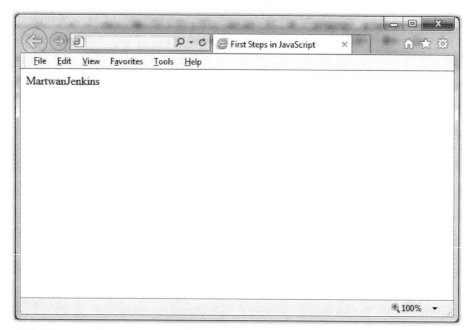

fg. 5 : Concatenating strings into a full name.

The value for `fullName` is `MartwanJenkins`. To make sure everything is in its proper form, you need to include the empty space as a string in quotation marks (*fg. 6*) :

```
var fullName = firstName+" "+lastName;
```

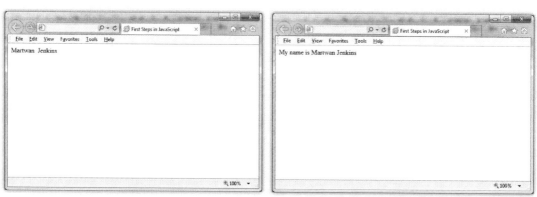

fg. 6 : Concatenating strings with spaces.   *fg. 7 : Concatenating a full sentence.*

Operators are also useful when you want to join text or combine variables. As a matter of fact, you can use this to construct more logical sentences. For example (*fg. 7*), you can combine the "My name is" text with a value from a calculated variable.

```
var firstName = "Martwan";
var lastName = "Jenkins";
var fullName = firstName+"
"+lastName;
document.write("My name is "
+fullName);
```

NOTE

When performing several mathematical operations in one statement, the rules of precedence apply.

Assignment Operators

Assignment operators are used to change variables within JavaScript. You are already familiar with the fundamental assignment operator, the equal sign (=), which is used to give an initial or a new value to a variable. Other assignment operators change the value of a variable, but they do this in a slightly different way.

For example, as the year passes you grow older and your age incrementally changes by one. To make this change in JavaScript, you can take several different approaches, all with the same results (*fg. 8*).

To play around with the possibilities of changing variables, try the following code that changes the value of the age variable displayed in the browser:

```
var age = 35;
document.write("<p>My age is "+age+"</p>");
age = age + 1;
document.write("<p>A year has passed, so now I am " +age+"</
p>");
age += 10;
document.write("<p>What? Are you telling me that I am a
grandad now? But I am only " +age+"</p>");
```

21

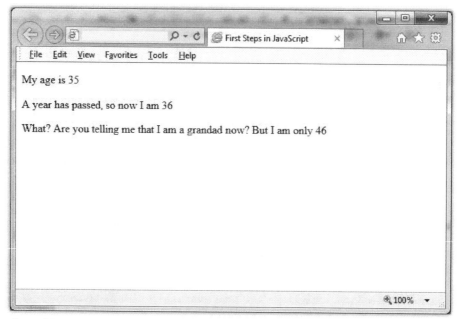

fg. 8 : Changing variables with assignment operators.

While at first these operations might appear slightly confusing, they are still logical if viewed from the programming angle. For example, if you read the statement `age=age+1` backwards, the value of 1 is added to the current age of 35, which would make 36 the new value of age. Additionally, you can use a complex assign operator such as (+=) in the statement `age+=10`, to increase the value of the variable by 10. You can also assign the same logic to other operations like subtraction, division and multiplication.

```
age-=5;        is the same as        age = age - 5;
age*= 5;       is the same as        age = age * 5;
age/=5;        is the same as        age = age / 5;
```

Additionally, when you want to increase/decrease the value of the variable by 1, you can also use the following assignment operators:

```
age++;         is the same as        age = age + 1;
age--;         is the same as        age = age - 1;
```

Comparison Operators

Like the name suggests comparison operators are used to compare two values. After the comparison is made, a value of either true or false is returned depending on whether the comparison was exact or not. Comparison operators are mostly used when evaluation conditions in loops or conditional statements, discussed in the next chapter.

The following table summarizes the most common comparison operators.

OPERATOR	MEANING	EXAMPLE	RETURN VALUE
==	equal to	4==4	True
>	greater than	3>4	False
<	less than	3<4	True
>=	greater than or equal to	4>=4	True
<=	less than or equal to	4<=5	True
!=	not equal to	3!=4	True

Logical Operators

Logical operators allow you to compare two or more conditional statements. The comparison lets you determine which statement is true so you can proceed accordingly. Just like comparison operators, logical operators return a value of either true or false, depending on the values on either side of the operator. The three most common logical operators are AND, OR and NOT.

The AND operator is represented by the `&&` code. The operator only returns a true value when the statements on both sides of the `&&` operator are true. If one or both statements are false, the operator returns a false value. This is in agreement with the rules of common language, for example, the statement "*This jacket has all the American colors, red, white and blue,*" is only true if the jacket has red (true), white (true) and blue (true). If only one of those colors is different (false), then the statement is also false. In JavaScript syntax, this would look something like the following:

```
(color1 = "red" && color2 = "white" && color3 = "blue")
```

The OR operator is represented by the || code. It returns a true value if the statement on one or both sides of the operator is true. The operator only returns a false value if both statements are false. For example, the statement *My brother will either go to Brazil or Thailand for his summer holiday* is true if my brother visited one (or maybe both) of those places.

```
(destination1 = "Brazil" || destination2 = "Thailand")
```

The NOT operator, represented by the ! code, is used to "claim" that the opposite statement is true. So, the operator returns a true value for any other condition than what is explicitly stated. For example, the statement *Brian does not weight 200 pounds* is true for any other value of weight except 200.

```
!(weight == 200)
```

You will learn the more practical aspects of logical operators in the next chapter, which focuses on conditional statements and loops.

Arrays

The variables examined up until this point can remember only a single piece of information at a time. However, more than often you need to keep track of multiple values like the months of the year or a shopping list. In such a case, JavaScript provides a nice way to remember multiple values under one variable, called an **array**. The following array variable holds the first six months of the year.

```
var months = ["January", "February", "March", "April",
"May", "June"];
```

When declaring an array variable you first use the `var` keyword followed by the name of the variable just like with regular variables. As the array contains multiple items, you need to provide a value for each item between opening and closing square brackets, [ ]. Like with normal variables if the value of the item is a string, you must place it within quotation marks. Otherwise, if the value is a number or possibly another variable, don't use any quotation characters. As an example, you can declare the following array of random items:

```
var randomItems = ["ball", -0.5, "black pony", 333, true]
```

It is also possible to define an empty array. You use the same syntax, but leave out the values for any item.

```
var hole = [];
```

Working with Array Items

Accessing array items is not the same as accessing common variables. Since an array holds multiple values, it is not sufficient just to use the name of the array variable. You also need to indicate its location within the array. The position of each item in an array is indicated by a number called an index. Therefore, to access an array item you have to use the array variable name and the index number. For example (*fg. 9*), if you want to display the first and the last item from your months variable, use the array name followed by a number enclosed in square brackets.

NOTE

JavaScript numbers each array item automatically. The index value for the first item is always 0, the index value for the second item is always 2, and so on.

```
var months = ["January", "February", "March", "April",
"May", "June"];
document.write(months[0]);
document.write(months[5]);
```

fg. 9 : Example for defining and displaying array results.

You use the index position when you want to change the value of a specific array item. For example, if in your `months` array you want to replace the name of the months with their shorthand, you can change each variable with the following statements:

```
months[0]  =  "Jan";
months[1]  =  "Feb";
months[2]  =  "Mar";
months[3]  =  "Apr";
months[4]  =  "May";
months[5]  =  "Jun";
```

Managing Array Elements

If you know the index value of the last array item, you can simply add more items by assigning values to subsequent items. For example, the following statement adds one more item in the array under the index value of 6.

```
months[6]  =  "Jul";
```

However, while programming you are almost never required to actually remember such trivialities as the last index value. Instead, to add one or more elements to the end of an array, you can use the keyword `push`. To add the final five months to your `months` array, combine the `push` keyword with the array name to form the following statement:

```
months.push("Aug", "Sep", "Oct", "Nov", "Dec", "Jan");
```

Well, it seems that you went over and added an extra month. To remove the last element of an array, use the pop keyword. As previously, you must combine the `pop` keyword with the array name to form the following statement:

```
months.pop();
```

This statement deletes the last array element, `"Jan"`, leaving you with an array containing all the months of the year.

When you want to add an element to the beginning of an array instead of the end, you can use the `unshift` keyword. Alternatively, when you want to remove an element from the beginning of an array, you can use the `shift` keyword. The following two statements add and subsequently remove a bogus first month to your array.

```
months.unshift("Sext");
months.shift();
```

If at any time you want to check the number of elements that are contained within an array, you can initiate the length property for the months array, `months.length`, and print it with the `document.write` statement.

To review all the different aspects you have learned, your complete code is (*fg. 10*):

```
var months = ["January", "February", "March", "April",
"May", "June"];
months[0] = "Jan";
months[1] = "Feb";
months[2] = "Mar";
months[3] = "Apr";
months[4] = "May";
months[5] = "Jun";
months.push("Aug", "Sep", "Oct", "Nov", "Dec", "Jan");
months.pop();
months.unshift("Sext");
months.shift();
document.write("The number of items in the array is: ",
months.length);
```

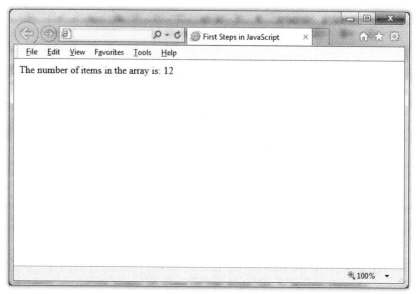

fg. 10 : Manipulating and displaying the array length.

Comments

From working with HTML and CSS you should already be familiar with comments. Basically, commenting is a way to tell the browser to ignore segments of the code. The purpose of comments is to leave notes about your code either for you or whomever is going to read the code after you. As JavaScript can be more difficult to understand when it is revised on a later date, commenting is even more important.

JavaScript recognizes two different approaches to commenting, marking a single line as a comment and marking multiple lines as comments. Regardless of the approach, the interpreter does not execute commented lines.

Single line comments are created with two forward slashes. When the interpreter finds two forward slashes, it ignores everything that follows until the end of the line.

```
//this is a single line comment
```

It is also possible to write a line that is part code and part comment. In the following example, after the variable year is declared, the rest of the line is treated as a comment.

```
var year = 2015; //this is most likely the current year
```

When you need more than one line of comments, you can use an alternative approach. Multiline comments in JavaScript are the same as multiline comments in CSS. The comments have a beginning, initiated by a forward slash and an asterisk (/*), and they have an end initiated by an asterisk and a forward slash (*/). The interpreter always ignores anything between these opening and closing comment signifiers.

```
/*This is a comment that
is written in exactly
three lines */
```

| 3 |
Conditional & Loop Statements

Creating a variable and storing a value in the variable is not really an accomplishment, neither is changing this variable with simple operators. To start making things interesting, your programs must react to users' actions and make them more intelligent. You can do this using conditional statements and loops.

Conditional Statements

You make a myriad of choices during your everyday activities: "*Should I get out of bed?*", "*What should I eat?*", "*Where should I go for coffee?*". These choices depend on the current situation, as the surrounding circumstances affect your decisions. In a similar fashion, JavaScript also has decision-making capabilities called conditional statements. Fundamentally, conditional statements are simple yes or no questions. If the answer is yes, the program does one thing, and if the answer is no, the program either does nothing or another thing.

The most basic conditional statement is the so-called `if` statement. This statement executes a task only if the answer to the question is true. To understand the syntax of an `if` statement, look at the following example:

```
var age = prompt("What is your age?"," ");
if (age > 30) {
document.write ("You are not so young anymore.");
}
```

The if statement consists of three parts. The if keyword indicates that what follows is a conditional statement. The parentheses, ( ), contain the yes/no question, also known as the condition. Finally, the curly braces, { }, contain one or more statements that need to be executed if the answer to the question is positive. Essentially, the { brace

31

marks the beginning and the } brace marks the end of the code that will be run if the condition is fulfilled.

In the previous example, the condition is a comparison between two values. With the condition (age>30) you check whether the age variable has a value greater than 30. If the condition is true, then the statement to write the text within the brackets on the web page is executed, otherwise, if false, the interpreter skips all of the statements within the curly brackets.

Alternative Conditions

In real life when one condition fails there is always an alternative. If the restaurant is out of cake, you can always order a fruit salad for dessert. Similarly, in JavaScript you also want something to happen when the condition is true and when the condition is false. To achieve this you can extend the if statement with an else clause. For example (*fg. 11*) :

```
var age = prompt("What is your age?", " ");
if (age < 18) {
document.write("You can enter the web site.");
}
else  {
document.write("You are too old to watch cartoons.");
}
```

In this example the user is asked to enter his or her age. Then the if statement evaluates whether the value of the age variable is less than 18. If this is true, the text *"You can enter the website"* is displayed on the page. If this condition is false, and the user has entered a value that is equal to or greater than 18, then the else clause is initiated and the text *"You are too old to watch cartoons"* is displayed on the web page.

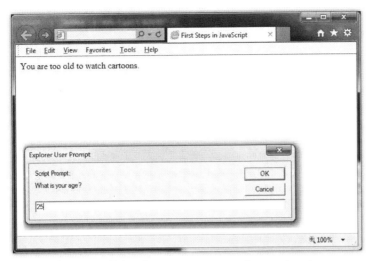

fg. 11 : Using a conditional statement to respond to user input.

To initiate an `else` clause you simply add it as a keyword after the closing brace of the conditional statement. The statement(s) that you want to execute are also placed in braces { }, as you have the option to add as many lines of code as necessary.

More often than not, there are more than two possible outcomes to a situation. When this is the case, JavaScript lets you use cascading `else if` statements to offer solutions to multiple alternatives. Start with an `if` statement for the first option, and then add one or more `else if` statements to trigger additional options. Like previously, the `else` clause is used in the end as the last alternative (*fg. 12*).

```
var money = prompt("How much money do you have in your
pocket?", " ");
if (money < 20) {
document.write("That is not enough. Go to the ATM to get
some more.");
}
else if (money == 20) {
document.write("Exactly 20? That's great, buy me a nice
burger meal.");}
else {
document.write("You shouldn't carry so much money around.
Give some to me.");
}
```

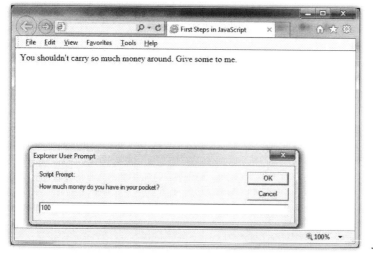

In this example, the user is asked to enter the amount of money he or she possesses. Afterwards, the JavaScript program assesses the answer and replies with one of three available responses based on the entered amount.

fg. 12 : Using alternative conditional statements.

Multiple Conditions

When dealing with different variables you need to form more complex conditional statements. For example (*fg. 13*), if you are having a private bachelorette party, you must make sure that you don't let people in unless they are female and over 18. Using the logical operators from the previous chapter and the else if conditional statements, you can build more intricate comparisons.

```
var gender = prompt("What is your gender?"," ");
var age = prompt("How old are you?"," ");
if ((gender == "female") && (age >= 18)) {
document.write("Please enter. Hope you brought a nice
gift.");}
else if (gender == "male") {
document.write("This is a bachelorette party. No guys
allowed.");
}
else {
document.write("You are probably too young to enter. Come
back in a few years.");
}
```

In this example you are making decisions based on two factors, gender and age. A positive decision is only available when both conditions are true: the person is a female over 18 years of age. In JavaScript, you combine conditions using logical operators, which in this case is the AND

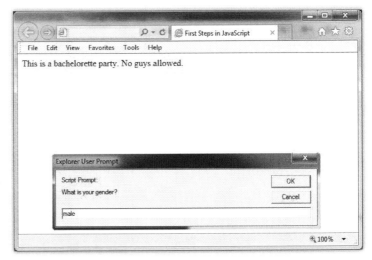

fg. 13 : Checking for multiple conditions.

operator represented by double ampersands (&&). When using this operator between two conditions within a single conditional statement, you summarize the outcome into only one condition.

Loop Statements

Some daily tasks are repetitive. To wash the dishes, you have to wash each dish separately. To climb down the stairs you have to step down one stair at a time. At the checkout counter, you have to take each item out of the cart, scan it and put it back in a bag. Well, in programming repetitive tasks are very easy to do. As a matter of fact, JavaScript is very good at performing repetitive tasks, as it has all the necessary tools to do the same thing over and over again. In programming lingo, repeatedly performing the same task is called a loop.

There are several different types of loops. They essentially do the same thing, but the approach is slightly different. This section familiarizes you with while loops and for loops.

While Loops

In a while loop, the same code is repeated as long as a certain condition is true. The following example checks your age as you grow every year.

```
var age = 1;
while (age < 18) {
        document.write("Another year has passed. You are
now "+age+" years old.<br>");
        age = age + 1;
}
document.write(age+"? Congratulations! You are now an
adult.");
```

After declaring the age variable, this example introduces a while statement. Following the while keyword, you place a condition between parentheses, which in this case is age<18. If the condition is true, the JavaScript interpreter runs the code that appears between the braces. Unlike a conditional statement, when the closing brace of the while statement is reached, JavaScript does not continue with the rest of the program but instead initiates the while statement again. As long as the number stored in the age variable is less than 18, the script runs the document.write() command.

When the condition is false, the interpreter 'exits' the loop and continues *parsing* the rest of the code. This makes the last line of the while loop very important. It not only changes the value of the condition variable, but it also makes it possible for the test condition to eventually be false. Without this possibility, you 'lock' the interpreter into performing the same task over and over again... forever. This is known as an infinite loop, which is essentially a loop that never completes. An infinite loop runs either until it crashes the computer or it receives a timeout from a modern interpreter after a certain period of time.

For Loops

In JavaScript there is a second option for creating a loop statement that is more compact and slightly more confusing. For loops can achieve the same thing as while loops with fewer lines of code, but the code is a bit unintuitive for the novice programmer. In a `for` loop, the variable declaration, the condition and the changing value of the variable are all done at the same time. In the following example (*fg. 14*), the previous age-growing while loop is written with a for loop syntax.

```
for (var age = 1; age < 18; age++) {
        document.write("Another year has passed. You are
now "+age+" years old.<br>");
}
document.write(age+"? Congratulations! You are now an
adult.");
```

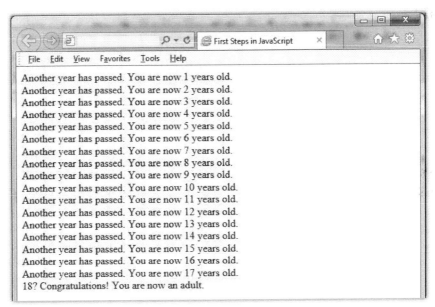

fg. 14 : An example of a for loop.

As evident from the image, the resulting content is exactly the same in both cases. Each loop begins with the `for` keyword. This is then followed by a set of parentheses that contains three parts:

1. The first part, which is applied only once at the beginning of the statement, declares the condition variable, `age`, and sets its initial value to 1. The initial value is used as a starting point for the number of times the loop repeats and can be any number. If this variable had been initialized earlier in the script, the `var` keyword would have been unnecessary.

2. The second part is the condition itself, which is evaluated every time before the loop is executed. As long as the condition is true, the `for` statement keeps repeating the code. When the condition is false, the loop is instructed to stop running, which in this example is when the `age` variable becomes greater than or equal to 18.

3. Finally, the third part determines the rate at which the condition variable is changed. In the example the condition variable increases by one after each cycle, but this is not mandatory. The condition variable can get larger or smaller and can increase or decrease by any amount you set.

To finish the structure of the for loop you use curly brackets to enclose the code that you want to use within the loop, which in the example is a line of text that is written on the web page with `document.write()`.

Loops & Arrays

Loop statements are very useful when you want do handle array variables. In JavaScript, you can use loops to cycle through array items, and when necessary, perform an action on each item.

Earlier in this book you created an array called `months` that contained the twelve months of the year.

```
var months = ["Jan", "Feb", "Mar", "Apr", "May", "Jun",
"Jul", "Aug", "Sep", "Oct", "Nov", "Dec"];
```

Using either a `while` or a `for` loop you can go through each item in the array and print it to the page. You can access the array items by using their indexes, then subsequently increase the index value in each loop cycle. If you use a while statement, you create the following code:

```
var counter = 0;
while (counter < months.length) {
        document.write(months[counter] + " ");
        counter++;
}
```

First, initiate a `counter` variable that has the same starting value as the index of the first array item, which is 0. Then, begin a `while` loop that runs until the `counter` value is less than the length of the array. The condition, `counter < months. length` inquires whether the current value of the `counter` variable is lower than the number of array items by comparing it to the array's length property. Each time the while loop runs, you print the value of a single array item and subsequently increase the value of the `counter` variable by 1.

If you want to perform the same action with a `for` loop you can use the following code (*fg. 15*):

```
var months = ["Jan", "Feb", "Mar", "Apr", "May", "Jun",
"Jul", "Aug", "Sep", "Oct", "Nov", "Dec"];
for (var counter = 0; counter < months.length; counter++)
{
        document.write(months[counter] + " ");
}
```

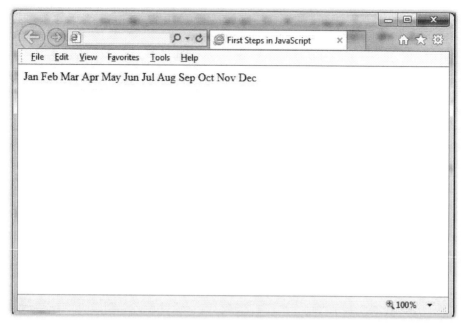

fg. 15 : Displaying array contents using loops.

| 4 |
Functions

When writing JavaScript code you are actually writing detailed instructions for what you want to happen one step at a time. In real life, you only need detailed instructions for the first time you perform the action. Afterwards you familiarize yourself with the steps and do the actions automatically. For example, remember the first time you used a touchscreen smartphone? To turn on the phone you had to perform two unknown actions: click a button to initiate the screen and swipe across the screen to unlock the phone. For each subsequent time you turned your phone on, you didn't need these instructions; you had already committed them to memory.

JavaScript has a similar mechanism that memorizes steps of a frequently used action, and this mechanism is called a function. A function is a series of steps you create in the beginning of your script in order to use it whenever you need those steps performed. You write the code only once and you run it whenever you need to.

This chapter explains the fundamentals behind using functions. You will learn what a function is, how to define and structure functions, and how to call functions in your scripts.

Creating Functions

The main purpose of a *function* is to perform a series of actions through a single command. The actual task that the function performs depends on the code itself. It can be something as simple as writing a single line of text in the browser or complex calculations that evaluate the final price of a shopping basket including discounts and shipping methods. Except for making your scripts more portable, functions are useful because they are reusable. Rather than rewriting blocks of code, you can use the function as many times as necessary. This becomes especially helpful when the functions are lengthy and perform complex tasks.

To define a basic function in JavaScript it is necessary to declare it with its name and code. The name of the function should indicate what the function does. The following example uses the keyword `function` followed by the function name `writeText` and a set of parentheses to declare a function:

```
function writeText() {
        document.write("The answer is 42.");
}
```

By using the keyword `function` you inform the interpreter that what follows is a series of steps that need to be remembered. The steps are listed between two curly braces, which mark the beginning and the end of the JavaScript code that is meant to be the function. In the example above, the steps are remembered as the name of the function, which is `writeText`. Hence, whenever you want to initiate this sequence of steps it is sufficient to only write out the function name followed by empty parentheses. This is also known as calling a function.

```
writeText();
```

In this basic example, every time you call the function within the main script, the text "*The answer is 42.*" is written on the web page. You can modify a previous script and create a function that checks the age of the user for a more precise example.

```
function checkAge() {
    if (age >= 18) {
document.write("You have reached the age of wisdom, please
enter and have some fun.");
    }
    else {
document.write("Please come back in a few years.");
    }
}
```

The JavaScript code that is placed in a function is stored in the browser's memory, waiting for you to call the function whenever you need to perform that specific action. In this example, the function checks how the age variable relates to the value of 18. As mentioned previously, to call the function you simply need to write out the name of the function followed by a pair of parentheses. You can also try adding a `prompt()` that asks the user to provide his or her age.

```
var age = prompt("How old are you?");
checkAge();
```

The complete script would be (*fg. 16*):

```
function checkAge() {
    if (age >= 18) {
        document.write("You have reached the age of wisdom,
please enter and have some fun.");
    }
    else {
    document.write("Please come back in a few years.");
    }
}
var age = prompt("How old are you?");
checkAge();
```

Additionally, you can use what you learned in previous chapters to make this function more intelligent. Instead of just receiving the answer "*Please come back in a few years,*" you can calculate the actual difference between 18 and the age the user entered.

To do this you introduce a variable named `difference` in the function, then calculate that difference as `18-age` if the entered value for age is less than 18, and finally print the `difference` variable along with the text.

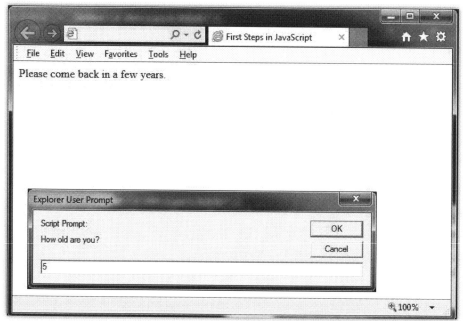

fg. 16 : Implementing a function to check the user's age.

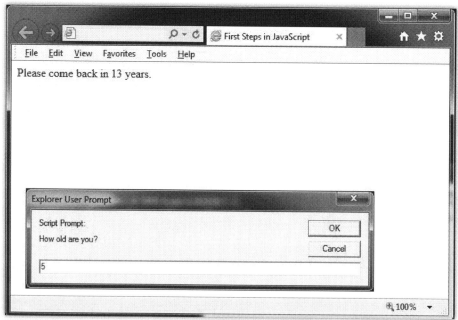

fg. 17 : Smart check age.

Adding this would look like the following (*fg. 17*):

```
function checkAge() {
     var difference;
     if (age >= 18) {
     document.write("You have reached the age of wisdom,
please enter and have some fun.");
       }
     else {
     difference = 18 - age;
     document.write("Please come back in "+difference+"
years.");
     }
}
var age = prompt("How old are you?","");
checkAge();
```

Sending Information to Functions

You can send one or more values to the function, thus increasing its versatility. When you send these values, the function is capable of processing this information before it comes back with an answer. The values you send are also known as arguments, while the process of sending information to a function is called 'passing an argument.' Once the argument is received, the function uses this data while carrying out the sequence of actions as specified in the code.

The basic syntax would look like this:

```
function functionName(argument) {
   //JavaScript code
}
```

Arguments are set on the first line of the function inside the set of parentheses, which you previously left blank. The values brought in as arguments automatically become declared variables within the function. These variables use the names given inside the parentheses and do not need to be further declared with the `var` keyword.

As the most basic example, the code below creates a function that shortens the syntax of the `document.write()` command (*fg. 18*).

```
function print(message) {
        document.write(message);
}
print("<p>What are you doing? document.write is a perfect
command.</p>");
print("<p>42 is the answer, but what is the question?</
p>");
```

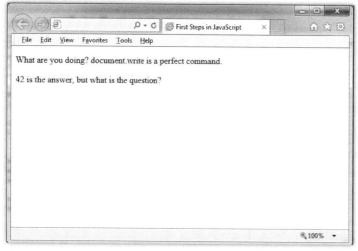

fg. 18 : Implementing a function to check the user's age.

This function, named `print()`, can accept one argument. When the function is called, this argument is passed on to the function and is stored as a variable named `message`. When the `document.write()` command is initiated within the function, it writes the contents of the message variable on the page. As mentioned previously, functions are not limited to processing single arguments. We can pass as many arguments to the function as needed as long as each argument is specified in the function and the function is called with the same number of arguments in the same order.

The following example (*fg. 19*) revisits the `checkAge()` function and makes it more versatile. It introduces the variables `name` and `years` to the function and has it respond with a personalized message.

```
function checkAge(name, years) {
if (years < 18) {
        document.write(name+" you are too young to
enter.<br>");
}
else {
        document.write(name+" you are above 18. Please come
in.<br>");
}
}
checkAge("Jack", 80);
checkAge("Alicia", 8);
checkAge("Simonetta", 15);
checkAge("Geronimo", 30);
```

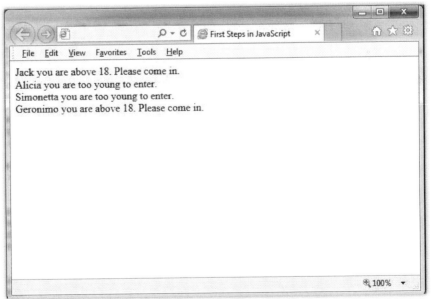

fg. 19 : Checking the ages for multiple users with a single function.

NOTE

You can send any type of JavaScript variable or value to a function: string, number, boolean, array, etc.

The previous example initiates the `checkAge()` function several times, each time with two different values, one for name and another for age. The first argument is stored as the name `variable`, and the second value is stored as the `years` variable. In the future, the `years` variable is used in a conditional statement to evaluate whether it is less than or greater than 18. Correspondingly, the `name` variable is used in the personalized message displayed through the `document.write()` command. To separate lines, you end each personalized message with a `<br>` tag.

Retrieving Information from Functions

Now that you have seen how to send information, you can "push" functions even further and get information back from them. To retrieve a value from the function to the main script you can use the return statement. The generic syntax looks like this:

```
function functionName(argument1, argument2) {
// JavaScript code
return data;}
```

For a more specific example assume that you want to learn the price of a product after a discount (*fg. 20*).

```
function checkPrice(price, discount) {
    var total = price - price * discount / 100;
    return total;
}
var actualprice = checkPrice(100, 20);
document.write("The   discounted   price   of   the   product
excluding VAT is "+actualprice)20
```

The checkPrice function accepts two values as arguments, the price of the product and the discount that needs to be applied. Once these valued are accepted they are stored in the price and discount variables respectively. The function then calculates the discounted price and

fg. 20 : Implementing a function to check the user's age.

assigns this calculated value to the variable `total`. The mathematical formula `price-price*discount/100` is just the formula used to make this calculation. Finally, the value for the variable `total` is returned to the main script with the `return` statement. What is passed down to the script is the value of the `total` variable, not the variable itself. In order to use this 'returned' value in the script, you need to store it inside a variable. The above example calls the `checkPrice()` function to calculate a 20% discount to a price of $100 and assigns the resulting value to the `actualprice` variable. This variable is then used in the main script and can be displayed on screen with the `document.write()` command.

You are not required to store the return value in a variable. You can also use it directly in the `document.write()` command.

```
document.write("The discounted price of the product
excluding VAT is "+checkPrice(100, 20));
```

Be aware that as soon as the browser's JavaScript interpreter encounters a return statement, it exits the function. This means that if there are any lines of code after the return statement, they will not be executed. Therefore, the return statement should be the last line of code within the function.

Local & Global Variables

For the JavaScript interpreter, the variables declared inside of a function are treated differently than variables declared outside of a function. The so-called 'scope' of the variables is different in each situation. The variables that exist inside a function are not visible to the rest of the script. They are valid only for the function itself. This means that function variables have a local scope. On the other hand, variables that are declared in the main part of the JavaScript code are meaningful to all parts of the script. This means that all existing functions in a script can access the variables that are created in its main body. These variables have a global scope.

To clarify the difference here are a few examples that calculate the number of drinks you have during a fun night out (*fg. 21*).

```
var drinks = 0;
function nightOut() {
        drinks = 5;
        document.write("Drinks in the function ", +drinks);
}
document.write("Drinks on the outside ", +drinks);
```

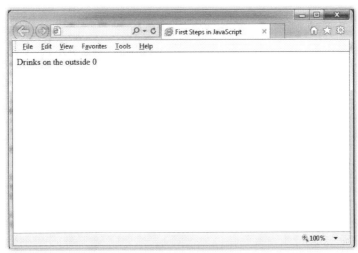

fg. 21 : Local vs. global variables example.

As you begin the day with 0 drinks, the variable `drinks` is declared in the main body of the JavaScript code with the assigned value of 0. As the `drinks` variable is declared in the main code, it has global scope, meaning that it is accessible to all other functions. For this reason, when you display this variable with the `document.write` statement both in the function and in the main code, you get the assigned value of 5.

Now, assume that you want to track the number of drinks at each place you visit with the following code (*fg. 22*):

```
var drinks=0;
var bardrinks = 0;
var clubdrinks = 0;
function nightOut() {
        var bardrinks = 3;
        var clubdrinks = 5;
        var drinks = bardrinks + clubdrinks;
        document.write("<p>Bar drinks in the function ",
+bardrinks);
        document.write("<p>Club drinks in the function ",
+clubdrinks);
        document.write("<p>Drinks in the function ",
+drinks);
}
nightOut();
document.write("<p>Bar drinks on the outside ",
+bardrinks);
document.write("<p>Club drinks on the outside ",
+clubdrinks);
document.write("<p>Drinks on the outside ", +drinks);
```

As in the previous example, the variable `drinks` is declared in the main body of the script, and, therefore, it has a global scope. However, this variation (*fg. 22*) also declares two additional variables, `bardrinks` and `clubdrinks`, within the function.

These two variables have a local scope and can be accessed only in the function itself. Hence, when you display these variables with the `document.write()` statement within the function you see values, while when you display these variables in the main code you don't see any values.

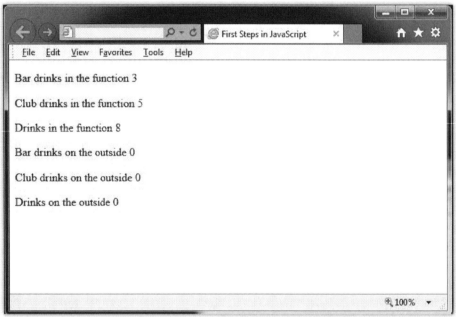

fg. 22 : Local vs. global variables extended example.

| 5 |
Objects

The real world is filled with objects, like cars, TVs, and dolls. Most of these objects are made up of many different parts and can also do one or more actions. The programming world, specifically JavaScript, is also full of objects.

This chapter takes your JavaScript knowledge to the next level and looks at the more advanced concepts starting with objects and object-oriented programming. Understanding these concepts will provide you with a vital set of tools that you can even apply when learning other programming languages.

What Are Objects?

To represent physical things and concepts in the programming world you need to use *objects*. But before you use programming objects, consider an object from the real world, for instance a car. If you want to describe a car, you talk about its characteristics such as color, make and model. You might expand your description to number of doors, seats, engine type, maximum speed or any other set of characteristics. You can also talk about how you use the car, from turning the ignition key to driving or listening to the stereo, or even how you use parts of the car, like reclining the seats. You can even compare different car "versions" based on this outline.

fg. 23 : Two identical cars.

In programming, the car is described as an object. The characteristics of the car such as color, make, model, are defined as the ***properties*** of the car object. The things you can do with the car, like driving or listening to music, are represented by what is known as ***methods***. And finally, each actual representation of a car is called an ***instance***. For example, in the previous image (*fg. 23*) you are looking at two instances of a car.

Creating Objects

There are two approaches to creating objects in JavaScript, you can either use an object ***constructor*** function or a literal notation. Start with an object constructor example:

```
var car = new Object ();
```

The first part of this statement is familiar; you use the `var` keyword to define a car variable. As you want to define the variable as an object, you use the new operator followed by the `Object()` constructor. This instructs JavaScript to create an empty object and assign it the name car.

Once the empty object has been created you can start defining its properties. Each property has a name and a value, with each name/value pair describing a particular instance of the object. For your car object you can assign the properties `color`, `make` and `model`.

```
var car = new Object();
car.color = "red";
car.make = "Ford";
car.model = "Mustang";
```

Notice that when defining properties you use the object name, followed by a dot, followed by the property name. This is known as dot syntax, in which the dot connects the property (or method) to the object.

To define a method for the object, you need to create a function that becomes a part of the object. To begin, create a simple method that displays a notification that the car has been turned on.

```
car.startCar = function () {
    document.write("The engine has started.<br>");
}
```

As you are familiar with functions, you can see that the `startCar` method is created with the `function` keyword, followed by a series of statements placed within curly braces. Since this code only creates the method, in order to see this method in action you have to call it in the script using the object name.

```
car.startCar();
```

The complete code would be (*fg. 24*):

```
var car=new Object();
car.color = "red";
car.make = "Ford";
car.model= "Mustang";
car.startCar = function () {
        document.write("The engine has started.<br>");
document.write("You are driving a "+car.color+" "+car.
make+" "+car.model);
}
car.startCar();
```

NOTE

You can always distinguish a method from a property by the parentheses. A method name always ends in parentheses.

fg. 24 : Defining a car object.

If you can use a function to create something, you can use a method, too, which means you can create anything you can imagine. You can even use a method to change the properties of the object itself. The following example creates a method that changes the color of the car.

```
car.changeColor = function (othercolor) {
    this.color = othercolor;
    document.write("The car is now "+this.color);}
```

Notice two differences from the previous method: you are passing an argument to the method using a new keyword, this. The keyword this refers to the object itself and allows you to assign new property values or even create new properties at the same time. The complete code is (*fg. 25*):

```
var car = new Object();
car.color = "red";
car.make = "Ford";
car.model = "Mustang";
car.startCar = function () {
    document.write("The engine has started.<br>");
    document.write("You are driving a "+car.color+"
"+car.make+" "+car.model);
}
car.changeColor = function (othercolor) {
    this.color = othercolor;
    document.write("<p>The car is now "+this.color);
}
car.startCar();
document.write("<p>The current color of the car is "+car.
color+ "<br>");
car.changeColor("green");
```

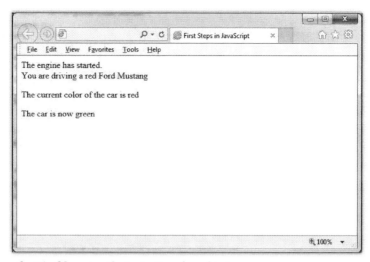

fg. 25 : Changing the properties of an object.

Another way to create objects in JavaScript is with object literal notation. With this approach you use curly brackets to enclose the properties and methods for the object.

The following code reproduces the car object with literal notation:

```
var car = {
color: "red",
make: "Ford",
model: "Mustang",
startCar: function () {
        document.write("The engine has started. <br>");
        },
changeColor:  function (othercolor) {
        this.color = othercolor;
        document.write("The car is now "+this.color);
        }
```

From the example it is noticeable that in literal notation each name/value pair is separated by a colon, including the method function. You can have as many name/value pairs as necessary as long as each pair is separated with a comma.

Unknowingly, you have been using JavaScript objects in your statements. For example, your most frequently used statement in all the examples is the `document.write()` statement. As a matter of fact in using this statement you have actually been addressing the document object and telling it to execute the `write()` method. You will learn more about the document object in the next chapter.

| 6 |

Document Object Model

In the previous chapter you learned how objects work and even looked at some of JavaScript's predefined objects. You are now prepared to investigate the most important web object, which is the document object. The document object primarily helps you gather information about the web page.

The browser creates the document object for each new HTML page. When it is created, JavaScript allows you access to a number of properties and methods of this object that can affect the document in various ways, such as managing or changing information. As a matter of fact you have been continuously using a method of this object, `document.write()`, in order to display content in a web page. Nevertheless, before exploring properties and methods you must first take a look at the Document Object Model (*DOM*).

Fundamental DOM Concepts

When the web browser receives an HTML file it displays it as a web page on the screen with all of the accompanying files like images and CSS styles. Nevertheless, the browser also creates a model of that web document based on its HTML structure. This means that all the tags, their attributes and the order in which they appear are remembered by the browser. This representation is called the Document Object Model (DOM), and it is used to provide information to JavaScript about how to communicate with the web page elements. Additionally, the DOM provides tools that can be used to navigate or modify the HTML code.

NOTE

For the code in this chapter to work, in some browsers you have to either put the `<script>` tag before the closing `</body>` tag or in an external .js file.

The World Wide Web Consortium (**W3C**) defined the Document Object Model standard that most browser developers use.

To better understand the DOM, first take a look at a very simple web page:

```
<!doctype html>
<html>
<head>
<meta charset="utf-8">
<title>Party Schedule</title>
<style type="text/css">
.current {
        color:red;
}
.finished {
        color:green;
}
</style>
</head>
<body>
<h1 id="partytitle">Party Plan</h1>
<ul id="partyplan">
   <li id="phase1">20:00 - Home warm-up</li>
   <li id="phase2">22:00 - Joe's Bar</li>
   <li id="phase3">00:00 - Nightclub 54</li>
</ul>
</body>
</html>
```

On a web page, tags wrap around other tags. The <html> tag wraps around the <head> and <body> tags. The <head> tag wraps around tags such as <title>, <meta> and <script>. The <body> tag wraps around all content tags such as

`<p>`, `<h1>` through `<h6>`, `<ul>`, `<table>` and so on.

This relationship between tags can be represented with a tree structure in which the `<html>` tag acts as the root of the tree while other tags represent different tree branch structures dependent on the tag hierarchy within the document. In addition to tags, a web browser also memorizes the attributes of the tag as well as the textual content within the tag. In the DOM each of these items, tags, attributes and text are treated as individual units called ***nodes***.

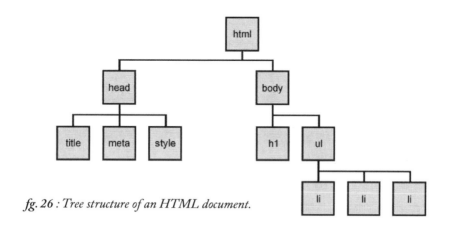

fg. 26 : Tree structure of an HTML document.

In the tree structure for this basic HTML page, the `<html>` element acts as a root element, while the `<head>` and `<body>` elements are nodes. In defining this relationship you can also refer to `<html>` as the parent node, and the `<head>` and `<body>` elements as child notes. In turn, both the `<head>` and `<body>` elements contain child nodes and so on. An item that contains no other child node terminates the tree structure at that node, which also known as a leaf node.

Selecting Document Elements

With the DOM structure in place, JavaScript can access the elements within the document in several different ways, depending on whether you want to select individual or multiple elements. In all approaches you first have to locate the node representing the element you need to access and subsequently use the content, child elements and attributes of that node.

Selecting Individual Elements

To select individual elements you most commonly use the `getElementById()` method. This method lets you select an element with a particular ID attribute applied to its HTML tag. This method is the most efficient way to access an element if you follow the presumption that the ID attribute is unique for every element within the page. The following example accesses the element whose ID attribute has the value `"phase1"` :

```
var firststop = document.getElementById("phase1");
```

Using the `getElementById()` method on the document object means that you are searching for the element with this ID anywhere on the page. Once the `"phase1"` element is assessed, which in your case is the first `<h1>` element, the reference to this node is stored in the `firststop` variable, and you can use JavaScript to make changes. The following example (*fg. 27*) assigns the attribute `class` with the value `"current"` to this element. You can include this code in a `<script>` tag in the `<head>` section.

```
var firststop = document.getElementById("phase1");
firststop.className = "current";
```

fg. 27 : Changing the style of a page element.

If you want to collect the text from a node, you can use the `textContent` property. More importantly, you can also use the `textContent` property to change the content of the node. In the following example (*fg. 28*) you first select the element that has the value `"partytitle"` in its id attribute and assign it to the `title` variable. Then you effectively change the text of this element by changing the `textContent` property of the `title` variable.

```
var title = document.getElementById("partytitle");
title.textContent = "Party Schedule";
```

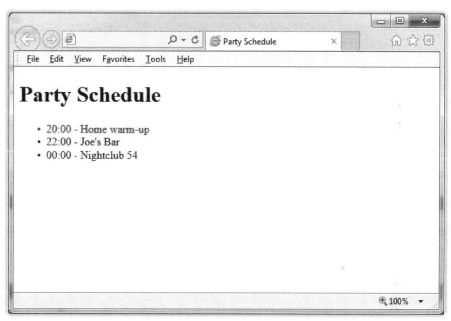

fg. 28 : Changing the content of a page element.

Selecting Group Elements

While sometimes selecting an individual element is sufficient, other times you may need to select a group of elements.

For example, you may need to select all `<li>` tags on a page or all elements that share a class attribute.

In these cases JavaScript offers the following two methods:

1. *getElementsByTagName()* : a method that lets you select every instance of a particular tag.

2. *getElementsByClassName()* : a method that retrieves all elements that share a particular class name.

Selecting a group of elements means that the method returns more than one node. This collection of nodes is known as a NodeList and is stored in an array-like item. Each node is given an index number, starting with 0, while the order of the nodes are in the same order in which they appear on the page. Although NodeLists look like arrays and behave like arrays, semantically they are a type of object called a collection. As an object, a collection has its own properties and methods that are rather useful when dealing with a NodeList. The following example selects all <li> elements and assigns their node references to the schedule variable.

```
var schedule = document.getElementsByTagName ("li");
```

If you want to access each element separately, you can use an array syntax:

```
var item1 = schedule[0];
var item2 = schedule[1];
var item3 = schedule[2];
```

However, when you select a group of items, you usually want to interact with the whole group. As an example (*fig. 29*), assign the class attribute with the "finished" value to all <li> elements. For this purpose you can use a loop to go through each element in the NodeList.

```
var schedule = document.getElementsByTagName ("li");
for (var i = 0; i < schedule.length; i++) {
    schedule[i].className = "finished";}
```

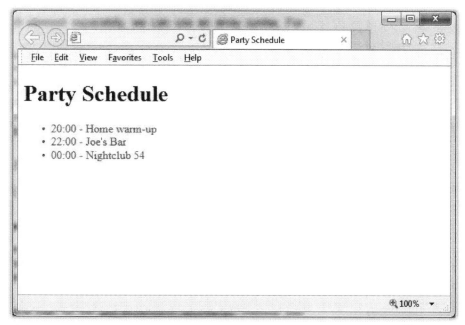

fg. 29 : Changing the class attribute for all <li> elements.

Similar to working with arrays, when working with collections you can use the length property to determine the size of the collection. You can then use this information in a for loop in order to effectively go through every NodeList item and assign the "finished" class attribute.

You can use exactly the same logic for the getElementsByClassName() method, which stores a NodeList in a collection and gives each node an index number. As with the getElementByTagName() method, you can access individual items and manage the collection through its object properties and methods.

Traveling Through the DOM

When you use any of the previously discussed methods to select an element node, you can also select other elements in relation to this element. This type of relative selection is considered an element property.

previousSibling & nextSibling

The previousSibling and nextSibling properties refer to adjacent elements on the same DOM level. For example, if you select the second <li>

element with the id value "phase2", the "phase1" <li> element is considered a previousSibling, while the "phase3" <li> element is nextSibling. In the case in which there is no sibling, (ex. the "phase1" element has no previousSibling), the value of this property remains null.

The following example selects the <li> element, which has "phase2" as a value for its id attribute, and changes the class attribute for both the selected element and its previous sibling.

```
var secondstop = document.getElementById("phase2");
var prevstop=secondstop.previousSibling;
secondstop.className = "current";
prevstop.className = "finished";
```

Parents & Children

You can also travel to different levels of the DOM hierarchy using the selected element as a starting point. If you want to move one level up, you can use the parentNode property. For example, if you have the second <li> element selected you can refer to its parent element, the <ul> element, with the following syntax:

```
var secondstop = document.getElementById("phase2");
var upperelement = secondstop.parentNode;
```

Alternatively, if you want to move one level down, you can use either the firstChild or the lastChild property. The following example selects the <ul> element with "partyplan" as a value for its id attribute. Using the firstChild property it refers to the first <li> element of this list, while with the lastChild property it refers to the last <li> element of this list.

```
var plan = document.getElementById("partyplan");
var child1 = plan.firstChild;
var child2 = plan.lastChild;
```

Adding & Managing Content

So far, this chapter has discussed how to find elements in the DOM. The more interesting aspects are the approaches to managing content within the DOM.

Changing HTML

The `textContent` property retrieves only text values and ignores the subsequent HTML structure. If you want to edit the page HTML, you have to use the `innerHTML` property. This property can be used on any element node and is capable of both retrieving and editing content.

```
var liContent = document.getElementById("phase1").
innerHTML;
```

When retrieving the HTML from the `<li>` element with `"phase1"` as a value for its `id` attribute, `innerHTML` captures the whole content of the element, text and markup, as a string variable. If you apply the same syntax for the `<ul>` element, the innerHTML property will capture all of the `<li>` items.

You can also use the `innerHTML` property to change the content of the element. If this content contains additional markup, these new elements will be processed and added to the DOM tree. For example (*fg. 30*), add the `<em>` tag to the first `<li>` item in the party list:

```
var firstStop = document.getElementById("phase1");
firstStop.innerHTML = "<em>20:00 - Home warm-up</em>";
```

DOM Manipulation

DOM manipulation is a more direct technique to managing document content. This is a 3-step process that uses the following methods:

1. *createElement()* : Create a new element node with the `createElement()` method. This element node is stored in a variable and it is not yet a part of the DOM.

2. ***createTextNode()*** : Create a new text node with the `createTextNode()` method. As in the previous step, this text node is stored in a variable and is not a part of the document.

3. ***appendChild()*** : Add the created element to the DOM tree with the `appendChild()` method. The element is added as a child to an existing element. This method can be used to add the text node to the element node.

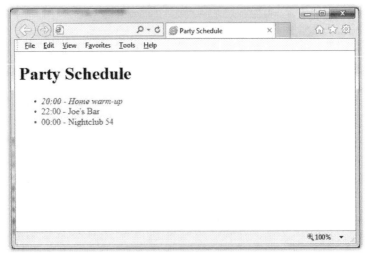

fig. 30 : Adding an <em> element with content to the first list item.

This example creates a new element that you can add to the existing party list. Use the `createElement()` method and add this element to the `newPlan` variable.

```
var newPlan = document.createElement("li");
```

Following, create a new text node and add its content as a value to the `newPlanText` variable.

```
var newPlanText = document.createTextNode("04:00 - Back
to home");
```

Now assign the content of the text node to the newPlan element using the appendChild() method.

```
newPlan.appendChild(newPlanText);
```

Finally, add this element to the list. Use the getElementById() method to select the list through its "partyplan" id, and apply the appendChild() method to attach the newPlan element to the list.

```
document.getElementById("partyplan").
appendChild(newPlan);
```

The complete syntax is as follows (*fg. 31*):

```
var newPlan = document.createElement("li");
var newPlanText = document.createTextNode("04:00 - Back
to home");
newPlan.appendChild(newPlanText);
document.getElementById("partyplan").
appendChild(newPlan);
```

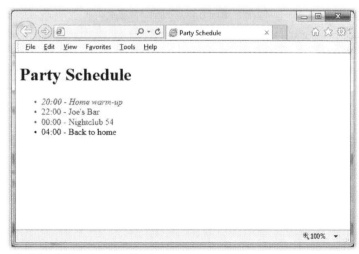

fg. 31 : Adding a new <li> element.

Using a similar process you can also use DOM manipulation to remove an element from the page. As an example, remove the <h1> element, which acts as the main page heading. You must first select the element through its id attribute with "partytitle" as its value and store that element node in a variable.

```
var removeHeading = document.getElementById("partytitle");
```

Next, you need to find the parent element, which acts as a container for the <h1> element, which in this case is the <body> element. You can either select this element directly or use the parentNode property of the previously selected element. In either case you need to store the parent element in another variable.

```
var containerForHeading = removeHeading.parendNode;
```

Finally, use the removeChild() method on the parent element in order to discard the element that you want removed from the page.

```
containerForHeading.removeChild(removeHeading);
```

The complete syntax is as follows (*fg. 32*):

```
var removeHeading = document.getElementById("partytitle");
var containerForHeading = removeHeading.parentNode;
containerForHeading.removeChild(removeHeading);
```

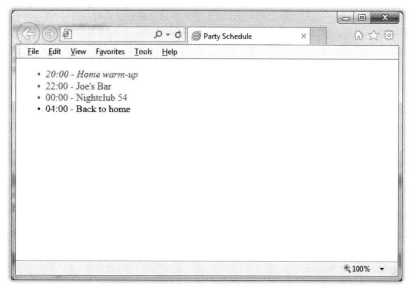

fg. 32 : Removed heading.

| 7 |
Events

One of the most important concepts in JavaScript is the use of events. An *event* is simply something that happens, like pressing a key on the keyboard or clicking somewhere on the page. As long as something happens and it has been expected, you can respond to it with a specific action. You can intercept the anticipated event and respond in kind by calling a function when that event occurs. As you will see in this final chapter, to make JavaScript anticipate events you use event handlers or event listeners.

Event Types

When you interact with web pages, you initiate a lot of events. You click a link, hover over an element, type text, open the browser, close a tab, copy/paste text, fill-out forms and so on. Almost everything you do triggers an event, and when an event is triggered you usually want to code a function that reacts specifically to that event.

There are many types of events to which you we can react, but you only need to focus on mouse events, keyboard events and browser/object events. The following three tables give brief descriptions of the most commonly used events for each event type.

Mouse events occur when the user does something with the mouse like moving, clicking, and dragging.

EVENT	DESCRIPTION
onclick	The user clicks an element
onbdlclick	The user double clicks an element
onmouseover	The user positions the mouse pointer on a specific element
onmouseout	The user moves the mouse pointer away from a specific element
ondrag	The user clicks and drags an element

Keyboard events occur either when a key is pressed or depressed.

EVENT	DESCRIPTION
onkeydown	The user is pressing a key
onkeyup	The user has released a pressed key

Browser/object events are more generic events that occur at different times like when the web page is loaded.

EVENT	DESCRIPTION
onload	The page/object has loaded
onunload	The page/object has unladed
onfocus	The page/element gets focus
onblur	The page/element loses focus
onerror	An error has occurred on the page
onresize	The page/object is resized
onscroll	The scrollbar of the page/object is used

Mouse events are the most common user-based events that occur on a web page. However, with the advent of touch-based devices there is an increased consideration for touch events.

NOTE

The full list of possible events is rather large and beyond the scope of this book. Please visit the W3C Schools web site for a complete list: (http://www.w3schools.com/jsref/dom_obj_event.asp).

Reacting to Events

In order to program JavaScript to react to an event you have to bind that event to an element on the page via event handlers. Event handlers let you indicate the event for which you are listening on any specific element. For this purpose there are three different approaches to event handlers:

1. *HTML event handlers* are attributes that can respond to events on the element to which they are added. Although still present in older web pages, this approach is no longer used as it integrates JavaScript into HTML when it should separate them.

2. *DOM event handlers* are introduced in the original DOM specification. They are separate from the HTML document and have a strong support in all major browsers. Their main drawback is the limitation of attaching only a single function to an event.

3. *DOM event listeners* are the favored approach to handling events and were introduced in an update of the DOM specification. They allow one event to trigger multiple functions, but they are not supported by IE8 and earlier versions of that browser.

When dealing with events you first have to select the element that will be the object of interaction. If for example this element is a link, then you need to specify the DOM node for that link element. After you have the element selected, you need to indicate the event that will act as a trigger. In programmer speak this is called "binding the event to the element node." Finally, you have to state the code, which is usually a function that you want to trigger when the event happens.

The remainder of the chapter focuses on event handlers and event listeners and ignores the discarded HTML approach. The examples in this chapter use a similar HTML structure like in the Party Schedule example from the previous chapter. The only difference is the link elements that have been added to every list item.

```html
<!doctype html>
<html>
<head>
<meta charset="utf-8">
<title>Party Schedule</title>
<style type="text/css">
.current {
    color:red;
}
.finished {
    color:green;
}
</style>
</head>
<body>
<h1 id="partytitle">Party Plan</h1>
<ul id="partyplan">
  <li id="phase1">20:00 - <a href="#" id="testLink">Home
warm-up</a></li>
  <li id="phase2">22:00 - Joe's Bar</li>
  <li id="phase3">00:00 - Nightclub 54</li>
</ul>
</body>
</html>
```

Event Handlers

There are many very similar approaches to using traditional DOM event handlers. Some are very compact, while others have more lines of code but might be more understandable. The following example is a brief script that changes the color of the link once it is clicked. To begin, first create the function that you want to trigger when the event occurs.

```
function linkClick(){
        this.className = "current";
}
```

The `this.className` property instructs the object calling on this function to set its `className` property to `"current"`. Now that you have your function in place, call on the object that will trigger the event using the `getElementById()` method and assign its element node to a variable.

```
var firstLink = document.getElementById("testLink");
```

As you have retrieved the reference to the element node, you can finally construct a proper event handler.

```
firstLink.onclick = linkClick;
```

The complete syntax is as follows (*fig. 33*):

```
function linkClick(){
        this.className = "current";
}
var firstLink = document.getElementById("testLink");
firstLink.onclick = linkClick;
```

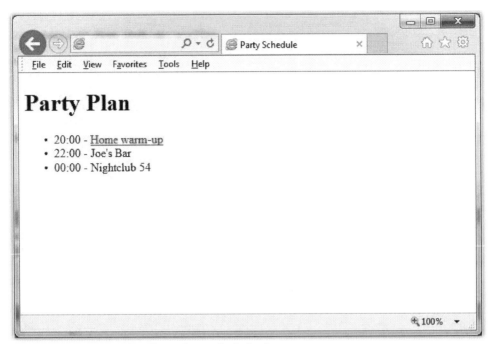

fg. 33 : Using an event handler to change the link color.

Considering that JavaScript is a very flexible language you can actually compact this in two lines of code, but you lose some of the flexibility.

```
document.getElementById("testLink").onclick = function
linkClick() {
    this.className = "current";
}
```

The linkClick function that is triggered by the onclick event doesn't have to be simple. You can change more than one property and even write complex scripts that deal with different situations. For example, the following code changes the text of the link and adds a class (*fg. 34*).

```
function linkClick(){
        this.className = "current";
        this.textContent = "Party Finished"
}
var firstLink = document.getElementById("testLink");
firstLink.onclick = linkClick;
```

No parentheses are added after the function name when the function is assigned to the event because if you used the linkClick() syntax with parentheses, you would be executing the function and assigning its value to onclick. When you don't use parentheses you assign the function (not the value) to the onclick property. You no longer control how the event handler function is executed, as the browser executes the function for you by automatically passing an Event object to the handler function.

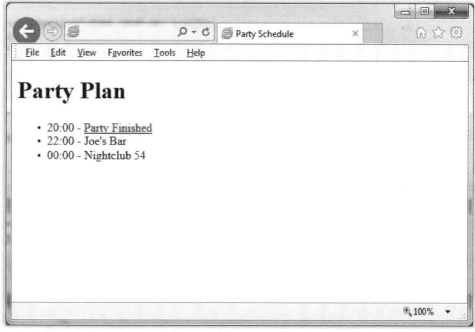

fg. 34 : Changing multiple properties on a click event.

Event Listeners

The more recent innovation to handling events is called an event listener. An event listener deals with multiple functions at the same time, although older browser support is lacking. The event listener is attached to the element via the `addEventListener()` method, which takes three properties.

The following example rewrites the previous code and changes the event handler to an event listener. The function remains the same.

```
function linkClick(){
        this.className = "current";
        this.textContent = "Party Finished"
}
var firstLink = document.getElementById("testLink");
firstLink.addEventListener("click", linkClick, false);
```

Instead of the event property, what is attached to the `firstlink` variable is the `addEventListener()` method. Within the parentheses you first have the event (without the preceding 'on'), followed by the name of the function and something called event flow. Event flow indicates the order in which the event is captured, and it is usually set to false.

summary

When you decide to learn something as complicated as JavaScript, there is a long process ahead of you. It is not sufficient to get acquainted with information; we have to apply that information in practical situations and real-life examples.

This book introduced the fundamental concepts of JavaScript and its approach to programming. You learned that JavaScript is a scripting language that enables you to enhance web pages by providing dynamic and interactive content. You looked into the process the browser follows when it interprets web pages, parsing the code element by element according to JavaScript instructions. You saw that JavaScript code is embedded into the web page itself, its presence marked with the `<script>` elements. Starting from the basic syntax and statement structure, in the second chapter you built up your knowledge of JavaScript's data types and variables. Particularly, you now know that JavaScript supports a number of types of data, such as numbers, text, and booleans. Numbers behave like numbers should, text is represented by strings of characters and is surrounded by quotation marks, and booleans are either true or false. These data types are stored in variables, committing their values to memory so they can be used later in your code. However, before giving value to a variable you are now aware that you must first declare its existence to the JavaScript interpreter. You also familiarized yourself with an array as a special type of variable that can hold more than one piece of data, which is managed by a unique index number.

The third chapter covered the core of the JavaScript language and its syntax. Specifically, you looked into decision-making with conditional statements and repetitive code use with loops. You learned that `if`, `else` and `else if` statements give the code its intelligence through the ability to make decisions. Determining whether a condition is true or false can help you decide on a course of action to follow, and in using the statements you can choose the block of code that will be executed respectively. Then you looped the code with while and for loops, as it is often necessary to repeat a block of code a number of times. You learned that looping requires initialization, condition testing, and increments in order to successfully execute blocks of code a specified number of times.

The fourth chapter finished looking at the JavaScript core scripting capabilities by observing functions as reusable bits of code. Although there are main built-in functions available, JavaScript enables you to define and use your own functions using the function keyword. You saw that functions can have zero or more parameters passed to them and can return a value if that is their intended purpose. In relation to functions, you learned about variable scope, in which variables declared outside a function are available globally while variables defined inside a function are private to that function and can't be accessed by the main code.

Chapter five moved on to the vital concept of objects. You learned that JavaScript is an object-based language as it represents things, such as strings, dates, and arrays using this object concept. You created new objects with the object constructor function or literal notation and also set the properties of those objects and defined their methods. You also learned how to access these properties and call these methods when needed.

Chapter six covered the DOM and how it offers means to access web page elements. You learned that the DOM represents the HTML document as a tree structure. You then learned how this tree structure makes it possible to navigate through its "branches" to different elements to use their properties and methods. You located element nodes to select individual elements and groups of elements. You then manipulated the content by either adding new elements or changing the existing structure.

You now have the basic knowledge and understanding to move on to learning more advanced concepts. You can use JavaScript to evaluate and interact with form data. To do this you also need to learn about serialization to translate the structure and information of the object. You can personalize the user experience by learning how to store information on local computers with cookies. You can push things further with AJAX, creating uninterrupted applications that don't require page refreshing for server communication. You can explore JavaScript frameworks such as jQuery or Modernizr to see how you can take JavaScript to its limit and easily create sophisticated high-class applications. Finally, you can learn how to create the perfect code with advanced error handling and using sophisticated debugging tools.

glossary

Argument -
A variable used by a function that has been passed to that function.

Array -
A collection of values in a single data type.

Boolean -
A data type accepting true/false variables.

Constructor -
A way to create a new instance of an object.

CSS -
Cascading StyleSheets.

DOM -
A collection of definitions that allow a program written in JavaScript to interact with the objects on the web page.

ECMAScript -
The core specification of the JavaScript language.

Event -
Something that happens on a web page.

Function -
A group of statements that have been collected together and given a name.

HTML -
HyperText Markup Language.

Instance -
A specific representation of an object.

JavaScript -
A scripting language allowing for improved interaction between users and web pages

Method -
A function attached to a particular object.
includes hyperlinks.

Node -
A unit representation from the DOM tree structure.

Object -
An individual item.

Operator -
A way to change/evaluate the content of a variable.

Parsing -
The process of reading the source code of the program in order to determine what the code is supposed to do.

Properties -
The characteristics of a particular object.

String -

A data type for text elements.

Variable -

A named location used for
storing values.

W3C -

World Wide Web Consortium.

about clydebank

We are a multi-media publishing company that provides reliable, high-quality and easily accessible information to a global customer base. Developed out of the need for beginner-friendly content that is accessible across multiple formats, we deliver reliable, up-to-date, high-quality information through our multiple product offerings.

Through our strategic partnerships with some of the world's largest retailers, we are able to simplify the learning process for customers around the world, providing them with an authoritative source of information for the subjects that matter to them. Our end-user focused philosophy puts the satisfaction of our customers at the forefront of our mission. We are committed to creating multi-media products that allow our customers to learn what they want, when they want and how they want.

ClydeBank Technology is a division of the multimedia-publishing firm ClydeBank Media LLC. ClydeBank Media's goal is to provide affordable, accessible information to a global market through different forms of media such as eBooks, paperback books and audio books. Company divisions are based on subject matter, each consisting of a dedicated team of researchers, writers, editors and designers.

For more information, please visit us at :
www.clydebankmedia.com
or contact *info@clydebankmedia.com*

Your world, simplified.

notes

STAY INFORMED

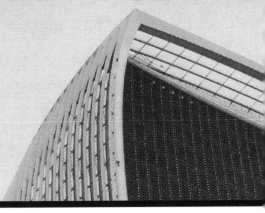

ClydeBank TECHNOLOGY | BLOG

Your Source for All Things Technology

Why Should I Sign Up for the Mailing List?

- Get a $10 ClydeBank Media gift card!
- Be the first to know about new products
- Receive exclusive promotions & discounts

Stay on top of the latest technology trends by joining our free mailing list today at:

www.clydebankmedia.com/technology-blog

Made in the USA
San Bernardino, CA
21 December 2017